TABLES OF CONTENTS

DAYBOOKS

of Critical Reading and Writing

G R E A T   S O U R C E

Grade 3

Grade 5

Grade 2

Grade 4

D1404174

DAYBOOKS
of Critical Reading and Writing

· · · · · · · · · ·

TABLES OF CONTENTS

Grade 2 ....page 1

Grade 3 ....page 4

Grade 4 ....page 7

Grade 5 ....page 11

Grade 6 ....page 16

TABLE OF CONTENTS

Grade 2

Lesson	Author/Literature	Focus/Strategy

INTRODUCTION

Active Reading
PAGES **7 – 12**

1. Mark the Reading	**Edward Marshall** from *Tuesday's Lunch* (FICTION)	
2. Predict What Happens		
3. Ask Questions		
4. Draw What You See		
5. Review		

UNIT 1

Reading Stories
PAGES **13 – 28**

1. Character Clues	**Jean Van Leeuwen** "Growing Up" from *More Tales of Amanda Pig*	*characters*
2. Where Are We?	**Cynthia Rylant** from *Henry and Mudge Under the Yellow Moon* (FICTION)	*setting*
3. What Is Happening?	**Angela Shelf Medearis** "The Scary Movie" from *The Adventures of Sugar and Junior* (FICTION)	*plot*

UNIT 2

Reading Nonfiction
PAGES **29 – 40**

1. Looking for the Main Idea	**Allan Fowler** from *The Sun Is Always Shining Somewhere* (NONFICTION)	*main idea*
2. Big Ideas and Small	**Melvin Berger** from *Germs Make Me Sick!* (NONFICTION)	*main idea/details*
3. What's It About?	**Paul Showers** from *Sleep Is For Everyone* (NONFICTION)	*retelling*

Lesson	Author/Literature	Focus/Strategy

U N I T 3

Reading Authors — PAGES **41 – 58**

1. Learning About Characters	**Wade Hudson** from *Jamal's Busy Day* (FICTION)	*characters*
2. Authors Choose Words	**Jama Kim Rattigan** from *Truman's Aunt Farm* (FICTION)	*word choice*
3. What a Problem!	**Arnold Lobel** from *"The Wishing Well"* (FICTION)	*plot*

U N I T 4

Reading Poetry — PAGES **59– 70**

1. Time...Dime...Rhyme!	**Mary Ann Hoberman** "Changing" (POETRY)	*rhyme*
2. This Poem Makes Me Feel...	**Walter Dean Myers** "Jeannie Had a Giggle" (POETRY)	*word fun*
3. Word Pictures	**Nikki Grimes** "Big Plans" (POETRY)	*word choice*

U N I T 5

Reading Nonfiction — PAGES **71 – 86**

1. What Does It Mean?	**Paula Z. Hogan** from *The Elephant* (NONFICTION)	*retelling*
2. Know What Happens	**Sabrina Crewe** from *The Alligator* (NONFICTION)	*sequencing*
3. Read to Understand	**Kimberly Brubaker Bradley** from *Pop! A Book About Bubbles* (NONFICTION)	*using graphic organizers*

TABLE OF CONTENTS Grade 3

Lesson	Author/Literature	Focus/Strategy

INTRODUCTION

Active Reading — PAGES **9 – 14**

1. Mark Up the Text — **Dick King-Smith** from *A Mouse Called Wolf* (FICTION)
2. Predict
3. Question
4. Visualize
5. Apply the Strategies — **Douglas Florian** "A Fire-Breathing Dragon" (POETRY)

UNIT 1

Reading Well — PAGES **15 – 30**

1. What Will Happen Next? — **William Steig** from *Solomon the Rusty Nail* (FICTION) — *predict*
2. What's the Big Idea? — **Stephen Kramer** from *How to Think Like a Scientist* (NONFICTION) — *main idea*
3. My Side of the Story — **Jon Scieszka** from *The True Story of the Three Little Pigs by A. Wolf* (FICTION) — *point of view*

UNIT 2

Reading Fiction — PAGES **31 – 44**

1. Character Clues — **Judy Blume** from *Freckle Juice* (FICTION) — *character*
2. Where Am I? — **Jean Van Leeuwen** from *Two Girls in Sister Dresses* (FICTION) — *setting*
3. What's Happening Here? — **Susana Sanromán** Senora Reganona (FICTION) — *plot*

Lesson	Author/Literature	Focus/Strategy

U N I T   3

Understanding Language PAGES **45 – 56**

1. Listening to a Poem	**Shel Silverstein** "Homework Machine" (POETRY)	*rhyme and rhythm*
2. Word Magic	**Aileen Fisher** "Cricket Jackets" (POETRY)	*word choice*
3. What's the Word?	**Jack Prelutsky** "I'm an Amiable Dragon" (POETRY) "The Multilingual Mynah Bird" (POETRY)	*context clues*

U N I T   4

Reading Authors PAGES **57 – 74**

1. Finding Out About Characters	**Beverly Cleary** from *Ellen Tebbits* (FICTION)	*character*
2. How an Author Writes	**Beverly Cleary** from *Henry Huggins* (FICTION)	*author's style*
3. Writing About Real Life	**Beverly Cleary** from *My Own Two Feet* (AUTOBIOGRAPHY)	*compare and contrast*

U N I T   5

Reading Well PAGES **75 – 90**

1. Why an Author Writes	**Arnold Lobel** from *Fables* (FICTION)	*author's purpose*
2. What's It All About	**Judy Hawes** from *Fireflies in the Night* (NONFICTION)	*main idea*
3. Using What You Know	**Ellen Schecter** from *Real Live Monsters!* (NONFICTION)	*prior knowledge*

Lesson	Author/Literature	Focus/Strategy

U N I T 6

Reading Nonfiction
PAGES **91 – 106**

1. Sum It Up	Robert Bateman from *Safari* (NONFICTION)	*summarize*
2. Tracking the Order of Events	David A. Adler from *A Picture Book of Hellen Keller* (BIOGRAPHY)	*sequence*
3. Reading Maps, Charts, and Graphs	Steve Jenkins from *Hottest, Coldest, Highest, Deepest* (NONFICTION)	*graphic aids*

U N I T 7

Understanding Language
PAGES **107 – 122**

1. Hey, Reader—Are Your Senses Awake?	Carolyn Lesser *Great Crystal Bear* (POETRY)	*sensory details*
2. Understanding Similies	Margot Theis Raven from *Angels in the Dust* (FICTION)	*simile*
3. When Animals Talk	Byrd Baylor from *Desert Voices* (POETRY)	*personification*

U N I T 8

Reading Authors
PAGES **123 – 137**

1. Characters Make the Story	Patricia McKissack "Monday" from *Ma Dear* (FICTION)	*character*
2. What's My Purpose	Patricia McKissack *Ma Dear*, Author's Note (NONFICTION)	*author's purpose*
3. An Author's Language	Patricia McKissack from *Mirandy and Brother Wind* (FICTION)	*author's style*

Grade 4 — TABLE OF CONTENTS

Lesson	Author/Literature	Focus/Strategy

INTRODUCTION

Active Reading — PAGES 7 – 13

Lesson	Author/Literature	Focus/Strategy
1. Mark Up the Text	Jane Yolen "The Lad" (FICTION)	
2. Visualize		
3. Predict		
4. Question		
5. Apply the Strategies		

UNIT 1

Reading Well — PAGES 15 – 28

Lesson	Author/Literature	Focus/Strategy
1. Getting the Big Picture	Ann Redpath from *Why Do We Laugh* (NONFICTION)	main idea
2. Reading into a Story	Patricia MacLachlan from *Sarah, Plain and Tall* (FICTION)	inference
3. Thinking Ahead	Josepha Sherman "Hare, Otter, Monkey, and Badger"	predict

UNIT 2

Reading Fiction — PAGES 29 – 44

Lesson	Author/Literature	Focus/Strategy
1. Who's Telling the Story?	Lawrence Yep from *Later, Gator* (FICTION)	point of view
2. Where Does the Story Take Place?	E.B. White from *Charlotte's Web* (FICTION)	setting
3. What Happens?	Cynthia Rylant "A Pet" (FICTION)	plot

Lesson	Author/Literature	Focus/Strategy

U N I T 3

Understanding Language
PAGES **45 – 58**

1. Creating Pictures with Words — **Gary Paulsen** / from *Cookcamp* (FICTION) — *descriptive language*

2. Comparing One Thing to Another — **Langston Hughes** / "Dreams" (POETRY) — *metaphor*

Andreya Renee Allen / "Black Is Beautiful" (POETRY)

Brandon N. Johnson / "Black Ancestors" (POETRY)

3. Stretching the Truth — **Mary Pope Osborne** / from *Davy Crockett* (FICTION) — *exaggeration* / *simile*

U N I T 4

Reading Authors
PAGES **59 – 70**

1. A World of Make-Believe — **Roald Dahl** / from *The BFG* (FICTION) — *fantasy*

4. Writing for Laughs — **Roald Dahl** / from *The Twits* (FICTION) — *humor*

5. Picturing a Magical Place — **Roald Dahl** / from *Charlie and the Chocolate Factory* (FICTION) — *descriptive language*

U N I T 5

Reading Well
PAGES **71 – 84**

1. Alike and Different — **Arnold Lobel** / from *Throw Your Tooth on the Roof* (NONFICTION) — *compare/contrast*

2. Asking Why — **Judy Hawes** / from *Fireflies in the Night* (NONFICTION) — *main idea*

3. Time Order — **Jean Craighead George** / from *One Day in the Prairie* (NONFICTION) — *sequence*

Lesson	Author/Literature	Focus/Strategy

U N I T   6

Reading Nonfiction
PAGES **85 – 98**

1. Skim First	**Steve Otfinoski** from *The Kid's Guide to Money* (NONFICTION)	*skim and scan*
2. Tell it Like It Is	**Stephen Kramer** from *Avalanche* (NONFICTION)	*summarize*
3. Using Graphic Aids	"Settling the Midwest" (NONFICTION-SOCIAL STUDIES)	*graphic aids*

U N I T   7

Understanding Language
PAGES **99 – 110**

1. The Power of Words	**Sid Fleischman** from *The Whipping Boy* (FICTION)	*word choice*
2. Is It Human?	**James Howe** from *Bunnicula* (FICTION)	*personification*
3. Onomato-*what?*	**Eve Merriam** "Weather" (POETRY)	*onomatopoeia*

U N I T   8

Reading Authors
PAGES **111 – 126**

1. That Could Be Me!	**Judy Blume** from *Otherwise Known as Sheila the Great* (FICTION)	*realistic fiction*
2. Thinking about Character	**Judy Blume** from *Tales of a Fourth Grade Nothing* (FICTION)	*characterization*
3. Making Connections	**Judy Blume** from *Fudgemania* (FICTION)	*connect to experience*

U N I T   9

Reading Well
PAGES **127 – 138**

1. Is It Important?	**Linda Hirschmann** from *In a Lick of a Flick of a Tongue* (NONFICTION)	*main idea/ supporting details*
2. It's up to You	**Gary Soto** from *Baseball in April* (FICTION)	*draw conclusions*
3. Is That a Fact?	**Dorothy Hinshaw Patent** from *Flashy, Fantastic Rain Forest Frogs* (NONFICTION)	*fact vs. opinion*

Lesson	Author/Literature	Focus/Strategy

U N I T   1 0

Reading Poetry — PAGES 139 – 148

1. What Does It Mean?	James Berry "Isn't My Name Magical?" (POETRY)	understand poetry
2. Word Pictures	Song Myong-ho "The Friend I Met While Running from the War (POETRY)	respond to poetry
3. Rhythm and Rhyme	Eloise Greenfield "Things" (POETRY)	rhyme and rhythm

U N I T   1 1

Understanding Language — PAGES 149 – 160

1. Word Clues	Janell Cannon from Verdi (FICTION)	context clues
2. Understanding Similies	Andrew Clements from Frindle (FICTION)	dialogue
3. When Animals Talk	Shel Silverstein "Sarah Cynthia Sylvia Stout Would Not Take the Garbage Out" (POETRY)	sensory language

U N I T   1 2

Reading Authors — PAGES 161 – 172

1. Folktales: Part of a Tradition	Julius Lester "What Is Trouble?" (FICTION)	folktales
2. Getting to the Heart of It	Julius Lester "The Knee-High Man" (FICTION)	theme
3. Understanding Characters	Julius Lester from Long Journey Home (FICTION)	characterization

Grade 5 — TABLE OF CONTENTS

Lesson	Author/Literature	Focus/Strategy

INTRODUCTION

Active Reading — PAGES 7 – 16

1. Mark Up the Text — Richard Peck "Three-Century Woman" (FICTION)
2. Predict
3. Question
4. Visualize
5. Apply the Strategies

UNIT 1

Reading Well — PAGES 17 – 32

1. Thinking Ahead — Joseph Bruchac "Little Hare and the Pine Tree" (FICTION) — *predict*
2. Reading Between the Lines — Jane Resh Thomas from *The Princess in the Pigpen* (FICTION) — *inference*
3. What's the Point? — Charlotte Jones from *Mistakes that Worked* (FICTION) — *main idea*
4. What Does It Mean to Me? — Jean Little from *About Loving* (FICTION) — *reflect*

UNIT 2

Reading Fiction — PAGES 33 – 46

1. In a Certain Time and Place — Frank Baum from *The Wizard of Oz* (FICTION) — *setting*
2. Who's Who? — Louis Sachar from *There's a Boy in the Girl's Bathroom* (FICTION) — *character*
3. What Happens? — Jean Craighead George "The Bird's Peace" (FICTION) — *plot*
4. What's the Message? — Jean Craighead George "The Bird's Peace" (FICTION) — *theme*

U N I T   3

Understanding Language
PAGES **47 – 62**

1. Expressing an Attitude — **Betty Bao Lord** / from *In the Year of the Boar and Jackie Robinson* (FICTION) — *tone*

2. Vivid Comparisons to Another — **Lillian Morrison** / "The Sidewalk Racer" (POETRY) — *metaphor*

3. Appearing Human — **Byrd Baylor** / "Desert Tortoise" (POETRY) — *personification*

4. Appealing to the Senses — **Kenneth Oppel** / from *Silverwing* (FICTION) — *sensory language*

U N I T   4

Reading Authors
PAGES **57 – 74**

1. What Would You Do? — **Phyllis Reynolds Naylor** / from *Beetles, Lightly Toasted* (FICTION) — *predict*

2. Recipe for Writing — **Phyllis Reynolds Naylor** / from *Beetles, Lightly Toasted* (FICTION) — *humor*

3. Conflict: It's Essential — **Phyllis Reynolds Naylor** / from *Boys Against Girls* (FICTION) — *conflict*

4. An Author's Style — **Phyllis Reynolds Naylor** / from *Shiloh* (FICTION) — *conflict*

U N I T   5

Reading Well
PAGES **79 – 94**

1. Getting the Whole Picture — **Andrea Warren** / from *Orphan Train Rider* (NONFICTION) — *main idea* / *details*

2. Summing It Up — **Sy Montgomery** / from *The Snake Scientist* (NONFICTION) — *summarize*

3. Asking Questions — **Gail LaBonte** / from *The Tarantula* (NONFICTION) — *ask questions*

4. Using Your Head — **Debbie and Tom Birdseye** / from *Under Our Skin: Kids Talk About Race* (NONFICTION) — *inference*

Lesson	Author/Literature	Focus/Strategy

U N I T 6

Reading Nonfiction — PAGES **95 – 112**

Lesson	Author/Literature	Focus/Strategy
1. First, Next, Last	Russell Freedman from *Lincoln: A Photobiography* (BIOGRAPHY)	sequence
2. In Your Own Words	Russell Freedman from *Lincoln: A Photobiography* (BIOGRAPHY)	summarize
3. Examining Cause and Effect and Graphs	Lynne Cherry from *A River Ran Wild* (NONFICTION)	cause/effect
4. Fiction Based on Fact	Elizabeth Yates "At-Mun" from *Amos Fortune: Free Man* (NONFICTION)	narrative nonfiction

U N I T 7

Understanding Language — PAGES **113 – 126**

Lesson	Author/Literature	Focus/Strategy
1. Playing With Words	Elizabeth Levy from *My Life as a Fifth-Grade Comedian* (FICTION)	word choice
2. Bringing Writing to Life	Cynthia Rylant from "Spaghetti" (FICTION)	imagery
3. The Writer's Style	Cynthia Rylant from "Spaghetti" (FICTION)	author's style
4. Descriptive Language	Natalie Babbitt from *Tuck Everlasting* (FICTION)	descriptive language

U N I T 8

Reading Authors — PAGES **127 – 140**

Lesson	Author/Literature	Focus/Strategy
1. What Next?	Avi from *The True Confessions of Charlotte Doyle* (FICTION)	predict
2. Conflict Between Characters	Avi from *The Barn* (FICTION)	conflict
3. Through *My* Eyes	Avi from *The Barn* (FICTION)	point of view
4. Identifying Author's Style	Avi from *The Blue Heron* (FICTION)	author's style

Lesson	Author/Literature	Focus/Strategy

U N I T   9

Reading Well
PAGES **141 – 154**

1. Skimming Can Tell You a Lot	**Steve Jenkins** from *Top of the World* (NONFICTION)	*skim*
2. Take Time for Graphics	"Spirit of Reform" from *We the People* (NONFICTION)	*reading graphics*
3. Note Taking: An Art	**Bill Nye** from *Bill Nye The Science Guy* (NONFICTION)	*taking notes*
4. What Does It Mean?	**Roald Dahl** from *Mathilda* (NONFICTION)	*context clues*

U N I T   1 0

Reading About Issues
PAGES **155 – 172**

1. Facts vs. Opinions	**James Haskins** "There Was a Time" (NONFICTION)	*fact/opinion*
2. Beware of Bias	**Patricia Thomas** "Loch Ness" (ARTICLE)	*bias*
3. Presenting Both Sides	"Schools Crack Down on Peanuts" from *Weekly Reader* (ARTICLE)	*pro/con*
4. Tone: It's Persuasive	**Ann McGovern** "Adventures in the Galápagos" (FICTION)	*tone*

U N I T   1 1

Understanding Language
PAGES **173 – 186**

1. Experiencing a Poem	**Gwendolyn Brooks** "A Little Girl's Poem" (POETRY)	*respond to poetry*
2. Giving Human Traits	**Nikki Giovanni** "Winter Poem" (POETRY)	*personification*
3. Striking Images	**Naomi Shihab Nye** "The Rider" (POETRY)	*imagery*
4. The Sound of a Poem	**Shel Silverstein** "Jimmy Jet and his TV Set" (POETRY)	*rhythm and rhyme*

U N I T   1 2

Reading Authors

PAGES **187 – 202**

1. The Role of Minor Characters — **Betsy Byars** from *The Pinballs* (FICTION) — *characterization*

2. Predicting a Character's Reactions — **Betsy Byars** from *The Cybil War* (FICTION) — *characterization*

3. Who's Telling the Story? — **Betsy Byars** from *Summer of the Swans* (FICTION) — *point of view*

4. A Sense of Humor — **Betsy Byars** from *Bingo Brown, Gypsy Lover* (FICTION) — *humor*

TABLE OF CONTENTS

Lesson	Author/Literature	Focus/Strategy

A N G L E S   O F   L I T E R A C Y

Angles of Literacy — PAGES 9 – 24

1. Becoming an Active Reader	Mildred D. Taylor, from *Roll of Thunder Hear My Cry* (FICTION)	
2. Connecting with the Story	Mildred D. Taylor, from *The Gold Cadillac* (FICTION)	
3. Language and Craft		
4. An Author's Perspective	Mildred D. Taylor, from *The Friendship* (FICTION)	
5. Focus on the Writer	Mildred D. Taylor, from an interview (NONFICTION)	

Essentials of Reading — PAGES 25 – 38

1. Thinking with the Writer	Ray Bradbury, "All Summer in a Day" (SHORT STORY)	*predict*
2. Reading Between the Lines	Ray Bradbury, "All Summer in a Day" (SHORT STORY)	*inference*
3. Managing the Main Idea	Mickey Roberts, "It's All in How You Say It" (NONFICTION)	*main idea*
4. Author's Purpose	Felice Holman, "Holiday Dinner" (POETRY)	*author's purpose*
5. Reflecting on Reading		*reflect*

S T O R Y   C O N N E C T I O N S

Essentials of Story — PAGES 39 – 54

1. A Story's Setting	Natalie Babbitt, from *The Search for Delicious* (FICTION)	*setting*
	Madeleine L'Engle, from *A Wrinkle in Time* (FICTION)	
2. A Story's Characters	Roald Dahl, from *Danny the Champion of the World* (FICTION)	*characterization*
3. A Story's Point of View	Roald Dahl, from *Danny the Champion of the World* (FICTION)	*point of view*
4. A Story's Plot	Richard Wilbur, "A Game of Catch" (SHORT STORY)	*plot*
5. A Story's Theme		*theme*

S T O R Y   C O N N E C T I O N S

Understanding Character
PAGES **55 – 72**

Lesson	Author/Literature	Focus/Strategy
1. A Character's Appearance	Isaac Bashevis Singer, "Utzel and His Daughter Poverty" (SHORT STORY)	*visualize*
2. A Character's Actions	Isaac Bashevis Singer, "Utzel and His Daughter Poverty" (SHORT STORY)	*characterization*
3. A Character's Speech	Paula Fox, from *One-Eyed Cat* (FICTION)	*inference*
4. A Character's Thoughts and Feelings	Paul Fleischman, from *Seedfolks* (FICTION)	*inference*
5. The Other Characters	Barbara Nichol, from *Beethoven Lives Upstairs* (FICTION)	*characterization*

L A N G U A G E   A N D   C R A F T

Author's Craft
PAGES **73 – 86**

Lesson	Author/Literature	Focus/Strategy
1. Surprising Comparisons	E. E. Cummings, "maggie and milly and molly and may" (POETRY)	*simile*
2. What It Is	Rita Dove, "Grape Sherbet" (POETRY)	*metaphor*
3. Almost Human	Aesop, "The Fox and the Crow" (FABLE)	*personification*
4. See It, Hear It, Feel It . . .	X. J. Kennedy, "Telephone Talk" (POETRY)	*sensory language*
5. It's a Twist	Shel Silverstein, "Almost Perfect" (POETRY)	*irony*

S H I F T I N G   P E R S P E C T I V E S

The Art of Argument
PAGES **87 – 98**

Lesson	Author/Literature	Focus/Strategy
1. What's It All About?	Steve Forbes, "A Uniformly Good Idea" (NONFICTION)	*main idea*
2. With Good Reason		*supporting details*
3. Seeing the Other Side	Rosa Velasquez, from "Robots Will Never Replace Humans" (NONFICTION)	*opposing viewpoints*
4. That's a Fact!		*fact and opinion*
5. Good Point?	Robert R. Halpern, from *Green Planet Rescue* (NONFICTION-SCIENCE)	*evaluate*

F O C U S   O N   T H E   W R I T E R

Focus on the Writer: Lois Lowry   PAGES **99 – 114**

1. Writing from Experience   from *A Summer to Die* (FICTION)

2. Tackling Tough Issues   from *A Summer to Die* (FICTION)

3. Painting a Picture   from *Autumn Street* (FICTION)

4. Making History Come Alive   from *Number the Stars* (HISTORICAL FICTION)

5. Where Do Stories Come From?   from Newbery acceptance speech (NONFICTION)

A N G L E S   O F   L I T E R A C Y

Challenging Reading   PAGES **115 – 128**

1. Using What You Already Know   **Margery Facklam,** from *And Then There Was*   *use prior knowledge*
                                  One (NONFICTION—SCIENCE)

2. Asking Questions   **Margery Facklam,** from *And Then There Was*   *formulate questions*
                                  One (NONFICTION—SCIENCE)

3. Adjusting Your Speed   **Kim-Hue Phan,** from "A Personal Narrative"(NONFICTION—SOCIAL STUDIES)   *change pace*

4. Putting Words in Context   **Alice Calaprice,** from *An Owl in the House* (NONFICTION—SCIENCE)   *use context clues*

5. Building Blocks of Words   **Robert Gardner,** from *Experimenting with Inventions*   *use structural clues*
                                  (NONFICTION—SCIENCE)

Active Reading: Social Studies   PAGES **129 – 142**

1. Coming Attractions   from *World: Adventures in Time and Place* (NONFICTION)   *preview*

2. It's What's Important   from *World: Adventures in Time and Place* (NONFICTION)   *highlight*
   That Counts

3. Keeping Track   **Elsa Marston,** from *The Ancient Egyptians* (NONFICTION)   *take notes*

4. To Sum Up   **Anne Steel,** from *Egyptian Pyramids* (NONFICTION)   *summarize*

5. Graphs, Maps, and More   **Anne Steel,** from *Egyptian Pyramids* (NONFICTION)   *use graphic sources*

S T O R Y   C O N N E C T I O N S

Active Reading: Expository Writing — PAGES **143 – 158**

1. Finding the Main Idea — **Spencer Christian**, from *Can It Really Rain Frogs?* (NONFICTION—SCIENCE) — *main idea*

2. Dealing with Details — *details*

3. Searching for Sequence — **Richard Wormser**, from *The Titanic* (NONFICTION-SOCIAL STUDIES) — *sequence*

4. Considering Cause and Effect — **Richard Wormser**, from *The Titanic* (NONFICTION-SOCIAL STUDIES) — *cause and effect*

5. Investigating and Inferring — **Phillip Hoose**, from *It's Our World, Too!* (NONFICTION) — *inference*

L A N G U A G E   A N D   C R A F T

Style and Structure — PAGES **159 – 172**

1. Words That Work — **Lucille Clifton**, "let there be new flowering" (POETRY) — *word choice*

2. Getting the Picture — **May Swenson**, "Waking from a Nap on the Beach" (POETRY) — *imagery/sensory language*

3. A Thumbprint of Words — **Jerry Spinelli**, from *Maniac Magee* (FICTION) — *author's style*

4. Setting the Pace — *text structure*

5. Structure and Meaning — **Edna St. Vincent Millay**, "The Courage That My Mother Had" (POETRY) — *text structure*

Active Reading: Poetry — PAGES **173 – 186**

1. The Poem on the Page — **Margaret Walker**, "Lineage" (POETRY) — *poetry terms*

2. Tuning In — **Gary Soto**, "Finding a Lucky Number" (POETRY) — *sensory language*

3. Beyond Words — **Mary TallMountain**, "There Is No Word for Goodbye" (POETRY) — *figurative language*

4. Word Music — **Ogden Nash**, "Adventures of Isabel" (POETRY) — *consonance and assonance*

5. The Beat Goes On — **Maya Angelou**, "Life Doesn't Frighten Me" (POETRY) — *rhythm, rhyme, repetition*

Lesson   Author/Literature   *Focus/Strategy*

S H I F T I N G   P E R S P E C T I V E S

Active Reading: Persuasive Writing   PAGES **187 – 202**

1. The Emotional Impact of Words   Nicolette Toussaint, "Hearing the Sweetest Songs" (NONFICTION)   *connotation vs. denotation*

2. Where Is the Writer Coming From?   Nicolette Toussaint, "Hearing the Sweetest Songs" (NONFICTION)   *author's perspective*

3. Taking Sides   Steven Levy, "The Myth of the Computer" (NONFICTION)   *bias*

4. Separating Fact from Opinion   *fact and opinion*

5. Tone   Robert Fulghum, from *All I Really Need to Know I Learned in Kindergarten* (NONFICTION)   *tone*

F O C U S   O N   T H E   W R I T E R

Focus on the Writer: Gary Paulsen   PAGES **203 – 218**

1. An Author's Style   from *The River* (FICTION)

2. Real-Life Characters   from *Dancing Carl* (FICTION)

3. Personal Challenges   from *Dancing Carl* (FICTION)

4. Challenges in Nature   from *Dogsong* (FICTION)

5. Autobiographical Writing   from *Woodsong* (AUTOBIOGRAPHY)

G R A D E   6   •   P A G E   2 0

Order Form

MAIL

Send this form to:

Great Source
Education Group
P.O. Box 7050
181 Ballardvale St.
Wilmington, MA 01887
Attn: Order Processing

FAX

Fax this form toll-free:
800-289-3994

PHONE

Place an order:
800-289-4490

Inquire about an order
or product:
800-289-4490
Monday-Friday
8:30am-6:30pm EST

GReaT SouRCe
EDUCATION GROUP
A Houghton Mifflin Company

TITLE	CODE	PRICE†	QTY.	TOTAL
Daybooks of Critical Reading and Writing				
Grade 2				
Student Book (5-Pack)	051991			
Teacher's Guide	050099			
Grade 3				
Student Book (5-Pack)	051992			
Teacher's Guide	048039			
Grade 4				
Student Book (5-Pack)	051993			
Teacher's Guide	048040			
Grade 5				
Student Book (5-Pack)	051994			
Teacher's Guide	048042			
Grade 6				
Student Book (5-Pack)	051996			
Teacher's Guide	046445			

†Please call 800-289-4490 for current prices.

All prices are subject to change without notice. All prices are F.O.B. point of origin and do not include shipping and handling charges.

* **Transportation/Handling:** Transportation and handling will be added to each order. For transportation and handling on school or district orders, customers should estimate 9% of order value. For individual orders, customers should refer to the "Orders from Individuals" chart in the Great Source catalog or call Customer Service at 1-800-289-4490 for assistance.

** **State Tax:** Applicable state sales tax will be added to your bill.

Merchandise Total	
Transportation/Handling*	
State Tax**	
GRAND TOTAL	

SHIP TO

School or Organization

Address

City   State   Zip

ORDERED BY

Name

Title

P.O. Number

Phone

Date of Order

BILL TO

School or Organization

Address

City   State   Zip

Attention

INDIVIDUAL ORDERS

◯ Payment Enclosed for $ _____

(Make checks payable to Great Source.)

Charge to:

◯ MasterCard   ◯ Visa   ◯ American Express

◯ Discover Card   ◯ Diners Club International

Account Number   Expiration Date

Authorized Signature (required for credit card purchases)

Date of Order

Daybooks of Critical Reading and Writing—now available for grades 2-12.

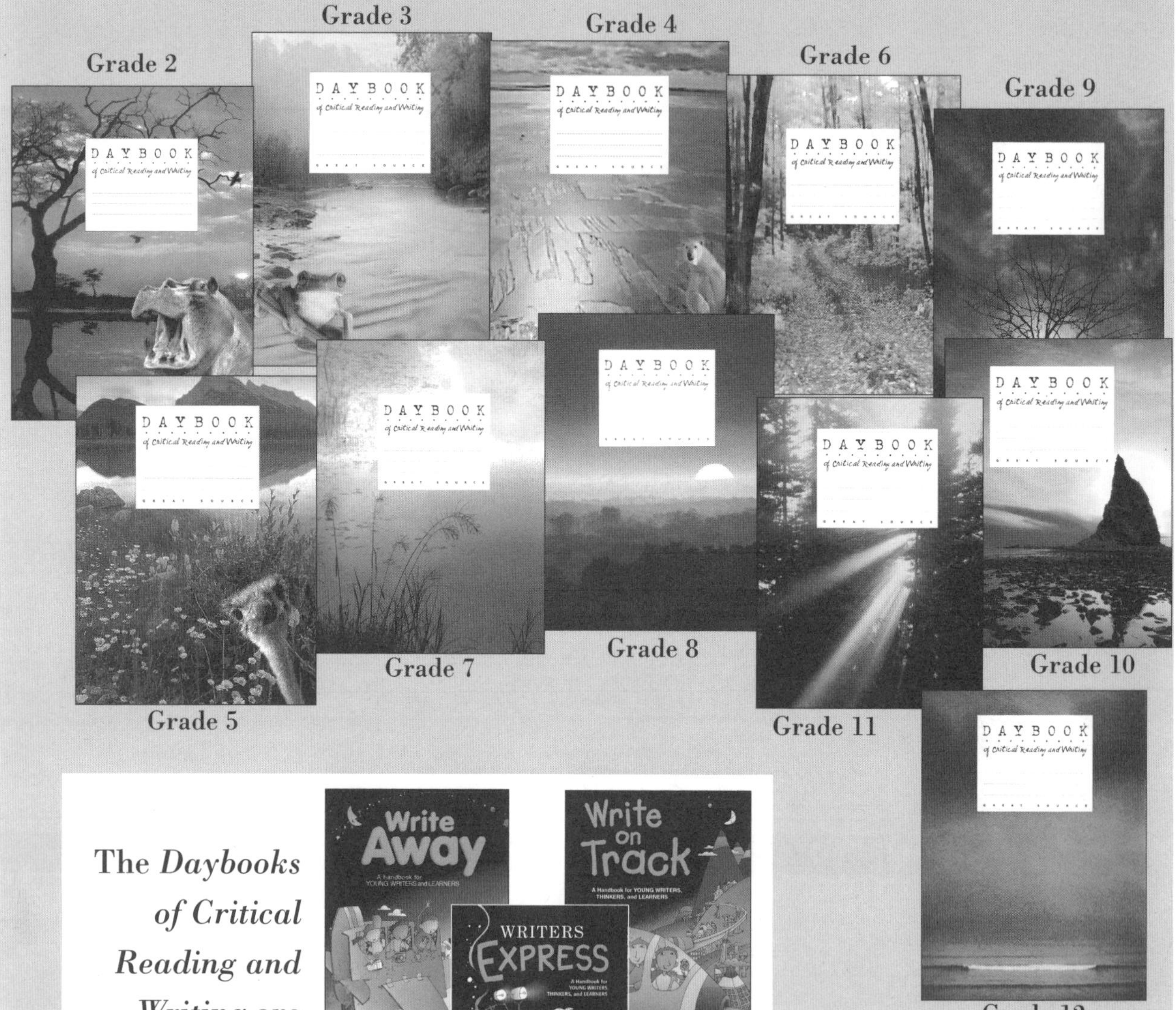

The *Daybooks of Critical Reading and Writing* are correlated to the best-selling Write Source writing handbooks.

ISBN 0-669-50700-8

9 780669 507003

GREAT SOURCE®
EDUCATION GROUP
A Houghton Mifflin Company

050700
2/05

For additional information, please call 800-289-4490.

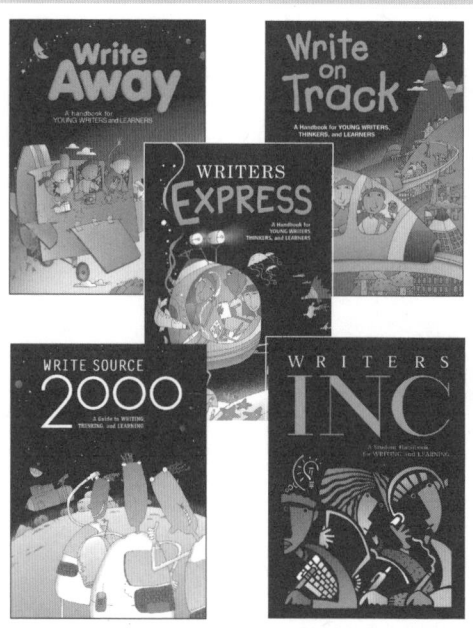

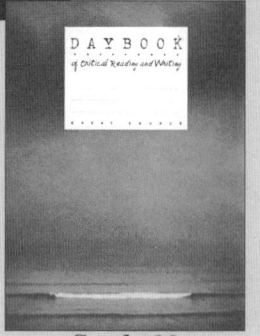